RAIL 4 PORTFOLIOS

The Peaks

Compiled by
Howard Johnston

Copyright © Jane's Publishing Company Limited 1985

First published in the United Kingdom in 1985 by
Jane's Publishing Company Limited
238 City Road, London EC1V 2PU

ISBN 0 7106 0340 1

Typeset by Netherwood Dalton & Co Ltd, Huddersfield

Printed by Netherwood Dalton & Co Ltd, Huddersfield

JANE'S

Cover illustrations

Front: The golden age of the Peaks is typified by this study of Class 45/1
No 45110 racing down from Sharnbrook summit on 31 October 1981
with the 1012 Sheffield-St Pancras. *(Rodney A Lissenden)*
Pentax 6x7 150mm Takumar Ektachrome 200 1/500, f6.3

Rear: No D21 (later to become 45026) in 'as built' condition passes
Duffield on 30 April 1966 with the 1215 Newcastle-Bristol express.
(Michael Mensing)
Nikkorex F 50mm Nikkor Agfa CT18 1/1000, f2.5

This page: Arrival of High Speed Trains on the East Coast Main Line
meant a rapid end to services such as this, 'The Yorkshire Pullman'
between Kings Cross and Harrogate, which made its final run on 5
May 1978. Distinctive even in later years by their reversed BR grey and
blue livery, the Metro-Cammell coaches passed into main-line
preservation in the hands of the Steam Locomotive Operators
Association. In their BR days, the Pullmans were increasingly
Peak-hauled as the years advanced — Toton-based 45110 (D73,
Crewe-built in 1960) passes Beeston Junction, Leeds on the up
'Yorkshire Pullman' on 1 July 1976. *(Gavin Morrison)*
Contaflex Tessar 50mm Kodachrome II 1/250, f3.5

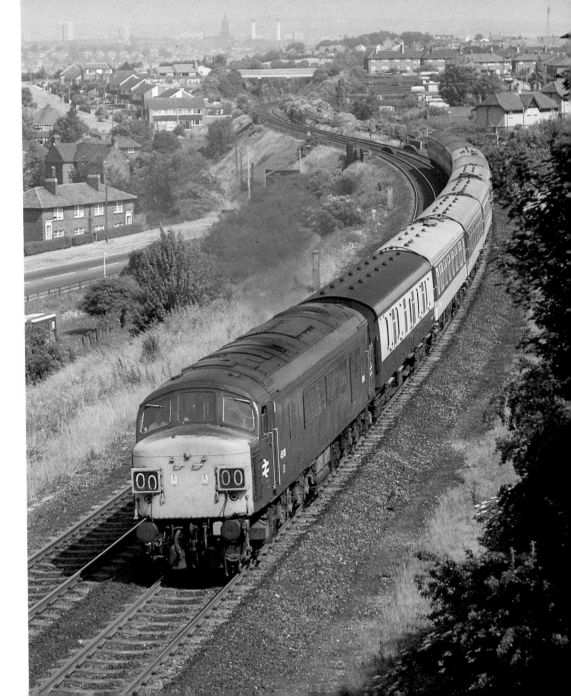

Introduction

Even to steam fans, the endless procession of grimy ex-WD 2-8-0s, LNER B1s and Standard 9Fs had little appeal as they plodded painfully across the flat fen landscapes of the GN & GE heavy freight route at the Lincolnshire-Cambridgeshire border. And when they went prematurely in 1962, their diesel replacements were the even more monotonous Brush Type 2s and English Electric Type 3s.

One day, it all changed. D8 *Penyghent*, one of the true prototype Peaks, was seen without any warning on a coal train through Spalding. The next day D2 *Helvellyn*, then D6 *Whernside*, and then the star of them all, D1 *Scafell Pike!* They had been newly allocated to Toton-Whitemoor duties and the uniqueness of appearance, names and perhaps above all the single-digit numbers left on us jaded platform-enders an impression the equivalent in cricket terms of England thrashing the West Indies by an innings and 200 runs . . .

Those magnificent ten were withdrawn years ago, and now the writing is on the wall for their 183 Class 45 and Class 46 successors, crafted in BR's own workshops at Derby and Crewe in only three years. Nothing startling or innovative, simply rugged and reliable.

Production was cut short when the more flexible Brush/Sulzer (Class 47) design came along, and the Peaks (as they were always nicknamed, never mind the regimental names) spent their lives being moved from pillar to post as modernisation swept them aside.

On the West Coast Main Line, it was electrification. On the Midland Main Line, North East/South West route and in the West Country, it was the High Speed Train. In the East Midlands, it was the arrival of bigger, more efficient Class 56s and 58s.

Cut by a third by the end of 1984, the Peaks still have a few freight strongholds, and regular passenger turns across the Pennines, coast to coast. And that's not counting the almost daily visits to Penzance, Norwich, Carlisle and Edinburgh. The Peaks are flexible friends.

'Real' Peaks *Great Gable* and *Penyghent* have survived into preservation; the Class 46s are a thing of the past; and the Class 45s will finally lose their lifeline when the East Coast route goes under the wires in the early 1990s.

The pictures in this book set out to demonstrate that the Peaks' travels have been truly nationwide. Sincere thanks are offered to the photographers who contributed so generously from their precious collections.

HOWARD JOHNSTON
Huntingdon
November 1984

The Peak outline is unmistakable in this late summer evening view of a Liverpool-Newcastle express climbing through Heaton Lodge Junction, Wakefield on 30 July 1979. The brief career of 46050 is already almost over. Brand new from Derby in November 1962 as D187, its mechanical failure at York in October 1980 dictated its withdrawal, and it was despatched to the Class 46 graveyard of Swindon for dismantling. (*Gavin Morrison*)
Pentax SP1000   Kodachrome 25   1/250, f3.5

The 44s

Top. Another few weeks, and D2, seen here nearly ready for painting at Derby on 23 May 1959, will be out running on Euston-Manchester expresses. Derby was the first BR workshop to abandon steam building completely in favour of diesel power, and the Peaks were an amalgam of operating experience obtained from the 1947 LMS prototype 10000, and a novel Sulzer 12-cylinder 2300hp power unit well tried on the Continent and shipped to the UK from Winterthur in Switzerland for installation in what would later be called the Class 44s. The second of the batch was named after Helvellyn in the Lake District, and its subsequent exploits are mapped out in later pages. (*R C Riley*)
Agfa Super Silette f2 Solagon Kodachrome 8 ASA

Left. The first two Peaks, D1 *Scafell Pike* and D2 *Helvellyn*, were built side by side at Derby Works from mid-1958 onwards. Delivery took place to Camden, but full West Coast Main Line running did not start until early 1960. This is D2 in original condition, without any form of front end yellow warning flash, already off the beaten track passing Canley Halt, west of Coventry with a Sunday morning Blackpool-Euston service on 16 April 1961. This train was diverted from the Trent Valley line because of electrification work, and reduced to a crawl by signal checks. D2 was itself soon diverted to other duties, as following pages explain. (*Michael Mensing*)
Retina IIa Xenon 50mm Agfacolor CT18 1/100, f8

Opposite. In dieselised East Anglia, it took scenes like this to rekindle enthusiasm in the railways. Their physical uniqueness made the ten Class 44s immediate favourites when they were transferred to the plodding Toton-Whitemoor coal trains, mostly returning light. Sunday 8 February 1970 was a busy day at Marholm, north of Peterborough, with three extra workings in the space of a couple of hours, and D8 *Penyghent* was still in largely as-built external condition (yellow warning panel added). Withdrawn in 1980 as 44008 this fine machine passed into preservation – compare this view with page 63. *(Colin Ding)* *Rolleiflex 80mm Planar High Speed Ektachrome 1/500, f5.6*

Left. Removal of the D prefix from BR's diesel fleet after the end of steam in 1968 saw nine of the Class 44s reduced to a single digit on their bodysides! *Cross Fell* thus became plain 5 until the TOPS computer numbering scheme caught up with it and 44005 became the style for its final years on those never-ending Toton-Whitemoor coal trains, one of which is the subject of this shot passing Spital, Peterborough, on 14 September 1973. Interesting bystander in the background is prototype Brush Type 4 No 1500, now better known as 47401.

Built at Derby in 1959 and allocated to Camden, *Cross Fell* was quickly relegated from top link work, but had a final passenger fling out of St Pancras on the first leg of the 'Peaks Express' railtour on 1 October 1977. Scrapping took place at Derby the following year. *(Colin Ding)* *Rolleiflex 80mm Planar Agfa professional 1/500, f5.6*

Top. Obviously low priority for a repaint, No 6 *Whernside* was the last member of Class 44 to stay in its original green livery. By now considerably work-stained after 12 years in service, it had however been further disfigured by the obligatory full yellow end which was arguably of little use if this dirty. Outshopped from Derby Works as a new passenger locomotive in the last few weeks of 1959, *Whernside* had spells at Camden, Derby and Carlisle before settling into the usual Class 44 routine from Toton, where this rare shot was captured on 31 March 1983. (*David Rapson*)
Praktica L   Agfa CT18 1/125, f5.6

Right. Saturday visitors to Toton in the later years could rely on seeing all serviceable Class 44s stabled at the front of the depot, and until the withdrawal of 44003 *Skiddaw* in July 1976 this could actually mean all ten. This side view of a pair of them there in May 1976 shows their body shape is identical with the later Class 45s and 46s. On the left, 44010 *Tryfan*, withdrawn that September but reprieved for another eight months' work, and on the right 44006 *Whernside*, whose career ended the same December after derailment at Spalding. Both were built, and dismantled, at Derby Works. (*Gavin Morrison*)
Pentax SP1000   Agfa CT18 1/250, f3.5

Top. The main line exploits of 44002 *Helvellyn* were long over when this photograph was taken along with 44009 *Snowdon* at Toton depot on 21 May 1978. Built at Derby in 1959 as D2, experimental uprating of its 12LDA28 power unit to 2500bhp was incorporated as a standard feature on the later 45s. *Helvellyn* was used for 100mph trials between Euston and Liverpool in the early 1960s as a prelude to electrification, but from then on it was drudgery of Toton-Whitemoor coal trains until withdrawal in February 1979. Final indignity for this famous loco was to be torn apart by souvenir hunters in Derby Works scrapyard during that October's open day. (*Hugh Ballantyne*)
Leica M3 50mm Summicron Kodachrome 25 1/60, f4

Left. A single Class 44 was a rare sight at York, let alone a coupled pair. Fear of imminent withdrawal in 1977 spawned a bevy of enterprising railtours, including one on 31 July which employed 1959-vintage 44002 *Helvellyn* and 44005 *Cross Fell* from Derby as far as York, where a Class 55 Deltic took over to Carlisle. Toton's finishing touch to two clean locos was the restoration for the day of the nameplates, removed a year earlier for fear of theft. 44005 only lasted another nine months, and was dismantled at Derby in December 1978. (*David Stacey*)
Pentax KX 50mm Kodachrome 25 1/125, f4.5

Peaks on the Midland

In its more anonymous days, split-headcode D71 rattles through the cutting a couple of miles north of Leagrave with the 1450 St Pancras-Leeds on a hot summer Sunday, 20 June 1965. The following May, this Crewe-built locomotive was selected to carry a regimental nameplate so complicated that punctuation is necessary – *The Staffordshire Regiment (The Prince of Wales's)*. A very early candidate also for blue livery, what has now become 45049 may well be one of the last of the class to remain in traffic as it was given a general overhaul at Derby Works in 1983,

against the run of play of most of the rest of the non-ETH Class 45s. (*Michael Mensing*)
Nikkorex F Nikkor 50mm Agfacolour CT18 1/1000, f2.5

Above. The paint was barely dry on ex-works D123 when it was turned out on the 1400 Manchester Central-Nottingham turn on 30 April 1966, demonstrating how smart the Peaks looked in their final green livery which preceded the corporate image blue. A close look (and comparison with the study on the back cover) will reveal that Derby's economy repaint by this stage does not include any embellishments. The

characteristic off-white stripe along the length of the lower bodyside and the painting of the bodyside grilles, was largely irrelevant anyway as they were quickly lost under the grime of normal service. This 1961 Crewe-built Peak next went into works in March 1974 and emerged with electric heat equipment, the new number 45125, and a virtual guarantee of immunity from withdrawal until the late 1980s at least. The location is half a mile south of Duffield, and this train has come off the now-closed Peak Forest route. (*Michael Mensing*)
Nikkorex F Nikkor 50mm Agfacolour CT18 1/100, f2.5

Peak experts have always been able to identify a Class 46 in recent years by an extra grille on the lower bodyside. The classic setting of the Midland Railway's 1868 London terminus of St Pancras is pure Peak, but the standard role of the Class 45 is taken here by a much scarcer and less popular 46018, deputising for a failed DMU on the Bedford run, the date 12 May 1980. All has changed – the electric wires are up, the DMUs have gone, and 46018 withdrawn. It was reprieved for an extra three years use from 1980, and was used at Stratford for spart parts before going back to Swindon works and the acetylene torch. *(Peter J Robinson)*
Pentax 6×7 Ektachrome 200 1/250, f8

Years of rumour about electrification of the Midland suburban system out of St Pancras finally became reality in 1983, and scenes like this, unchanged in the best part of a century, were suddenly transformed by the erection of masts and overhead wires, and replacement of time-honoured semaphores with MAS. Through Leicester, Nottingham and Sheffield services lost their Peak haulage at the same time to faster but indistinctive HSTs. 21 May 1977 was a hot day for 45120 (D107, Crewe 1961) tearing through Elstree with an up express. (*John S Whiteley*)
Pentax 135mm Takumar
Kodachrome 25 1/250, f3·5

11

Above. January 1 1976 was a black day for railway photographers and signalmen in boxes with glass windows in that it saw the discontinuation of locomotive route indicator panels. Locomotives such as this unidentified Class 45/1 have since lost them completely in favour of a less attractive flush front end. This was Chesterfield on 1 September 1975 before the HST revolution on the Midland Main Line that brought little extra speed, but more passenger business. (*John S Whiteley*)
Pentax 135mm Takumar Kodachrome 25 1/250, f4

Right. Sharnbrook summit, 60 miles out of St Pancras on the Midland Main Line, and 45139 is working hard on the northbound side with a nine-coach Mark 1 football special on 31 October 1981. (The climb is less taxing nowadays of course, because HSTs have a built-in banker at the rear . . .) 45139 started life as D109 at Crewe Works in June 1962, was fitted with ETH equipment for Midland duties in 1974, and can now be seen practically anywhere. (*Rodney Lissenden*)
Pentax 6×7 Ektachrome 200 1/500, f8

12

Electrification promises to sweep this scene away eventually. No 45123 *The Lancashire Fusilier* needs every one of its 2500 horse power to accelerate past the Midland Railway design signalbox at Kettering with the 1605 Nottingham-St Pancras on 9 June 1982. This locomotive was one of eighteen Class 45s built out of sequence when Crewe Works took on a batch originally intended for Derby. It was the third such machine, delivered as D52 in June 1962, converted to electric heat in 1974, and refurbished for an extended life in 1983. (*Hugh Ballantyne*)
Leica M4-2 Summicron 50mm Kodachrome 25 1/250, f2.8

A railway junction doesn't have to be protected by a signalbox nowadays, as shown by this immaculate but lonely view of Foxlow Junction on the Sheffield avoiding line north of Staveley. The box went in the summer of 1983; locomotive 46035 at the head of the steel coil train outlived most of its Class 46 sisters to survive into 1985 as a Derby research locomotive. Interestingly, it was allocated to Gateshead new as D172 in July 1962, and never moved away in its revenue-earning career. Date of this shot is 9 September 1983. (*John Chalcraft*) *Mamiya 645   80mm Agfa R100S*

Left. Royal Signals – not a name to honour a semaphore gantry with a regal association, but a military regiment. 45144, the locomotive bestowed with the title in June 1965, is one of only nine Class 45/1s with nameplates, many of them now vandalised like this one. Built at Derby Works as D55, *Royal Signals* has been at this familiar location a thousand times. How many gas holders like this one next to the St Pancras approaches have served as a backcloth to a locomotive portrait? Since this May 1976 view, the site has been disfigured by electric masts, 45144 has been given a general overhaul at Crewe and lost its centre headcode panel, and the Peaks have all but disappeared from this

stamping ground. (*Les Nixon*)
Pentax 6×7   105mm Takumar   Agfa CT18 1/250, f4.5

The 46s

Above. Crompton Parkinson's inability to meet BR's extraordinary demands for transmission deliveries led Brush to provide electrical equipment for Peaks D138-193, thereby creating the series that became Class 46. As with their later Class 45 sisters, the centrally-fitted headcodes applied to the 46s were progressively removed because of metal fatigue and replaced with a flush plate holding two sealed beam lamps. A solitary unmodified Class 46, No 46037, sur-

vived into 1984 with its headcode panels still in place, and was thus very much a celebrity until its spectacular demise in a cloud of smoke and flame north of the Lickey Incline on 16 June while working the 1035 Penzance-Leeds. Nineteen years earlier, the same locomotive was very much more run of the mill, bearing green livery (and an accumulation of grime!) in its guise of D174, hauling the 1516 Newcastle-Liverpool through the now-closed Arthington station on the Harrogate-Leeds line. The date, 17 July 1965. (*Michael Mensing*)
Nikkorex F   Nikkor 50mm   Agfacolor CT18 1/500, f3.2

Left. There was still practically a full complement of Gresley Pacifics at Gateshead when the depot took delivery of its first 2500hp Sulzer Type 4 diesel, D166, from Derby Works in the first week of May 1962. Their success was such that within four years steam was completely eliminated from main line workings. Compare this shot of an immaculate D166 therefore at Berwick-on-Tweed on the down 1A30 'Heart of Midlothian' on 30 May 1962 with those elsewhere in the book of the rundown wrecks that comprised the Class 46 fleet at the end of their working lives, ending with condemnation of

survivors 46025/7/35/45 on 25 November 1984. As for D166, it spent its entire career based in the North East, renumbered 46029, withdrawn as surplus in 1983, and consigned to Swindon for breaking up. *(Michael Mensing)*
Hasselblad 1000F   80mm Tessar
High Speed Ektachrome   1/1000, f3·5

Above. Introduction of any new type of locomotive is followed by the inevitable period of crewtraining, and Derby-built Class 46 D188 (46051) was loaned from Gateshead to the Leeds area in the latter part of 1963 for this purpose. Vintage

hauled stock is apparent in this view of D188 approaching Wortley Junction (Leeds) on an up working from Neville Hill depot to Appleby on 20 September. Re-organisation of North East/South West workings saw this locomotive allocated to Bristol Bath Road from 1973, but contraction of their numbers saw 46051 despatched back to Gateshead three years later. It was finally condemned in November 1983 and dismantled at Swindon Works. *(Gavin Morrison)*
Contaflex   50mm Tessar   Agfa CT18
1/500, f3·5

Above. 46056 was the final Peak off the Derby production line in January 1963, although mechanical parts had been ordered for another 20, which were to have been numbered D194-99, D1500-12. While Crewe finished its Class 45 order, the traction equipment was redirected to the Brush works at Loughborough to build what are now designated Class 47. 46056, ex-D193, was photographed at Brampton on 20 March 1982, having completed the lion's share of the 0718 Edinburgh-Newcastle-Carlisle. It was withdrawn later in the year and sent to Swindon for dismantling. (*Peter J Robinson*)
Pentax 6×7   Ektachrome 200   1/500, f5.6

Right. Colour photography seems worth the persistence when the outcome is such as this – 46023 at Brandon, County Durham with loaded coal hoppers from Widdrington bound for Bowaters at Sittingbourne, Kent. On the date in question, 29 October 1981, 46023's crew were not to know how close their steed would be to eventual total destruction. Delivered from Derby as D160 in April 1962, it saw spells on the LMR, NER and WR before withdrawal in full operational order in 1983. Sold in turn to the Central Electricity Generating Board along with sister 46009, it was earmarked as reserve loco to be smashed into a nuclear flask at 100mph. On the day of the tests, 17 July 1984, 46009 was smashed up, 46023 was reprieved. (*Peter J Robinson*)
Pentax 6×7   Ektachrome 200   1/1000, f4

Above. With Deltics for company, the less powerful and less revered Gateshead Class 46s were rarely out of the shadows on the East Coast route. BR had already decided to phase out the Peak design by the time this shot of 46039 passing Finsbury Park as a stand-in on a Kings Cross-Cleethorpes working was taken on 13 September 1980. This machine, the former D176, spent its entire career working from the North East bar six months at nearby Haymarket, and was withdrawn on October 23 1983, next stop Swindon. *(Geoff Cann)*
Pentax MX   50mm Kodachrome 64   1/500, f4

Right. Cambridgeshire is hardly noted for its scenic beauty, and passengers on the East Coast Main Line would be forgiven for dozing off. On 31 October 1981 however they would doubtless be looking at their watches as the Deltic-rostered 1403 Kings Cross-York was running 35 min late by St Neots, and the replacement loco 46001 was clearly ailing as well. (It was in fact withdrawn just eight weeks after this shot was taken.) Most of the interesting signalling features on this stretch of the ECML were swept away in 1978, and it will be further disfigured soon by electrification. *(Rodney Lissenden)*
Pentax 6×7   150mm   Ektachrome 200   1/500, f8

Top. Class 46s had the same 90mph top speed as the rest of the Peaks, but would "take a lifetime to get there" according to Midland crews who regarded them as distinctly inferior beasts. To blame were the Brush traction motors installed by Derby Works when D138 (46001) onwards were constructed from 1961 onwards. Many of the 46s migrated to NE/SW duties, and the effects of the 1980s recession and HST investment programme made then obvious withdrawal candidates. No 46001 went in December 1980 as part of the Laira clearout, but was resurrected from mothballs at Swindon nine months later. Needless to say, as this shot of a shabby 46001 at York depot on 29 September shows, the long spell standing in the rain played havoc with both bodywork and electrics. It was condemned again after just 12 weeks, and this time there was no reprieve. It was broken up at Swindon in July 1982. (*David Stacey*)
Pentax KX 50mm
Kodachrome 25 1/125, f4.5

Right. Suddenly it happened. BR's decision at the end of 1980 that it could no longer sustain the crippling effects of the recession saw scores of unwanted locomotives consigned to Swindon Works for storage – and that included a third of the entire Class 46 fleet. For these three Gateshead examples the recall never came. Nos 46043/2/1 (D180/79/78 of 1962) were withdrawn in October and November, and were broken up virtually where they stood. The date of the photograph is 5 December 1980. (*Howard Johnston*)
Olympus OM1 50mm
Ektachrome 64 1/125, f5.6

Opposite. How a solitary Class 46 came to be named when there were scores of 45s to choose from is lost in the mists of time. Fortunate recipient was 46026, built at Derby in April 1963 as plain D163, and named *Leicestershire and Derbyshire Yeomanry* the same month. Transferred to the WR in 1971 and the ER in 1980, it survived two months at the Swindon dump, and its drift into decreptitude was arrested by Gateshead depot staff who repainted it and renamed it in a special ceremony. There were still signs of the ornamental red they applied on the buffer beam under the returning grim at Holgate Junction, York on 11 August 1983, when it was stabled awaiting work with sister 46014. Withdrawal came in November 1984 but much-expected preservation didn't happen. Instead it was on tow to Doncaster for breaking up. (*Fred Kerr*)
Pentax 6×7 90mm
Agfa RS100 1/250, f5.6

The North East/South West route

Left. The Peaks held a near monopoly in NE/SW services until the early 1980s, when High Speed Trains brought new luxury to certain services. In 1984 examples were still to be seen on the residual locomotive-hauled traffic, especially the summer Saturday dated trains.

Twenty-one years earlier D27 scurried through Dunhampstead, near Worcester, on a Leeds-Cardiff working, demonstrating how attractive green diesel was with chocolate and cream BR Mark 1 stock. Built at Derby in 1961, this locomotive was one of the shorter-lived Peaks: renumbered 45028, it was withdrawn as run down and surplus when BR hit a financial low ebb at the end of 1980. It was consigned to Swindon for disposal.

Although, avoiding lines such as that by-passing Worcester, on which Dunhampstead is located, are unfashionable nowadays because traffic is sufficiently sparse to make them uneconomic to maintain, Worcester itself, stifled since the mid-19th century by Midland and Great Western rivalry, still misses out to some extent as many NE/SW services avoid the town centre by this shorter route which comes no closer than three miles. *(Michael Mensing)*

Voigtlander Bessa II
105mm Color-Heliar
High Speed Ektachrome
1/500, f5.6

Right. A scorcher at Cheltenham, and with hindsight the transition of the NE/SW route to diesel traction does not appear unattractive. Nostalgia plays tricks however, as most photographers turned their backs on green Peaks and their "drab" maroon stock. Twenty years later, preservationists rush to copy this style! This was D15, eighteen months out of Derby Works, on a Newcastle-Bristol working on 29 August 1962, and sporting a Neville Hill steam-style shedplate on its front end. Renumbered to 45018 it was one of the shortest-lived Class 45s, condemned in January 1981, and dismantled at Swindon later the following year. *(Derek Cross)*

Linhof Technika   100mm Zeiss
Agfa CT18 Professional   1/250

Right. Instant history. Although taken as recently as 21 May 1977, this rustic scene only a stone's throw from the centre of Birmingham has been transformed for the better (from the rail point of view of course) by the opening of the new University station. Locomotive is 46017, Derby-built D154 of February 1962 which pioneered East Coast Peak duties when it became the Finsbury Park crew-trainer. The rest of its 24-year career was equally hectic with transfers between Midland, Western and Eastern Regions and almost the whole of 1981 in store at Swindon. Withdrawal came in April 1984 after a mishap. The train in the picture is a Swansea-Manchester service.
(Michael Mensing)
Bronica S2A
135mm Nikkor   Agfachrome
1/800, f5.6

Opposite. The colour shot that all photographers dream of — the freak humidity that produces a full-hue rainbow and its reflection just as an express is due. The date, 7 June 1977, was part of the Silver Jubilee Bank Holiday, and a fine day turned showery as the afternoon progressed before a last burst of sunshine in late evening. It was 8.07pm when split-headcode Peak 45020 stormed past the site of Ashchurch station, Gloucestershire with the day's Penzance-Birmingham. Starting life at Derby Works as D26 in early 1961, it later migrated to Eastern Region depots of Neville Hill, York, Holbeck and finally Tinsley, and minus its headcode panels was still in active use at the end of 1983, albeit minus its steam-heat boiler. *(Michael Mensing)*
Bronica S2A
75mm Nikkor
Agfachrome 50S (160ASA)
1/1000, f3.2

Top. Toton depot staff came up with the idea of giving their Class 45 fleet a little of their old external sparkle when they came in for heavy repair work from 1980 onwards. Sadly, only two Class 45/1s, Nos 45110 and 45121, had received white stripes on the upper and lower bodysides before the Toton men were told to desist, and they returned to their dull former selves upon works overhaul. Complete with black front end marker lights as well, a highly burnished 45121 (D18, Derby 1960) was a stirring sight emerging from the York station overall roof on 30 May 1981 with Brush Class 31/4 31405 and the Sheffield-Clifton ecs in tow. (*Barry Plues*) *Pentax SP1000 50mm Agfa CT21 1/250, f4*

Right. A pair of cross-eyed Peaks at Gloucester Horton Road depot in August 1977. Prior to removal and replacement by sealed beam lamps, the headcode blinds in the Peaks' front ends were taken out, and white dots on black backgrounds inserted into the illuminated boxes – and not always quite straight, as this view of two of the split-headcode variety, 45053 and 45021, demonstrates excellently. No 45021 on the right (built as D25 at Derby in April 1961) was withdrawn at the end of 1980, and scrapped at Swindon; 45053 meanwhile escaped from the Swindon dump for renovation at Crewe in 1982, but the temptation to remove parts for other Class 45/1 overhauls was too great, and its remains were still awaiting disposal at the end of 1984. The former D76 (Crewe 1960) it was the last to keep its split headcodes. (*Barry Nicolle*) *Pentax SP2 50mm Agfa CT18 1/125, f8*

Identical externally, the Class 45 and 46 Peaks represent two stages in the development of the Type 4 locomotive off BR's own production lines at Derby and Crewe Works. Although 20-odd years of operation have seen many alterations made to the specification, the principal difference is the use of Crompton Parkinson traction motors in the Class 45 and Brush in the 46, a seemingly pointless equipment variation which stemmed from BR's decision to acquire transmissions from two sources in its haste to get the Peaks into traffic. The CP motors proved the most reliable and efficient in traffic, helping the type's longevity. It is Sunday lunchtime at Newcastle Central on 10 February 1980, and 46049 (D186, Derby November 1962) has arrived light to relieve 45041 *Royal Tank Regiment* (D53, Crewe June 1962) on the 1238 departure to Plymouth. The 46 was withdrawn on 12 December 1983, and sent to Swindon for breaking-up. The 45 was also a candidate for withdrawal in 1985. (*Peter J Robinson*)

Pentax 6×7 Ektachrome 200 1/125, f11

31

Peaks on the WR

Above. Night-time at Bristol Bath Road, where the Peaks consolidated their already major foothold as the diesel-hydraulic influence waned. The front end modifications carried out from 1974 are clearly seen in this night shot. 45020 (D26, Derby 1961) on the left has had its headcode panel replaced by a flush metal sheet, including an extra handrail on the earliest conversions. Behind it is 45071 (D125, Crewe 1961), first to be modified after accident damage and since withdrawn. On the right, 45019 (D33, Derby 1961), headcodes intact. The date: 20 April 1979. (*Geoff Cann*)
Praktica STL 50mm Tessar Kodachrome 64 16sec, f5.6

Right. The majesty of Exeter St David's frames the flagship of the Class 45 fleet, 45060 *Sherwood Forester*, at the head of the 1023 Manchester-Plymouth on 29 September 1976 (Class 33 33002 is alongside). Prior to computer renumbering, *Sherwood Forester* carried the number D100, and was selected in September 1961 as the first Peak to bear regimental nameplates, a similar name being removed simultaneously from its 'Royal Scot' 4-6-0 predecessor 46112. The LMR has never let this locomotive be transferred away, but by 1984 few remembered its significance. Indeed, one nameplate and both regimental crests had been stolen from its bodysides. (*Hugh Ballantyne*)
Leica M3 50mm Summicron Kodachrome 25 1/250, f5.6

32

Left. The elevated vantage point, reballasted track and up-to-date stock gives this study a thoroughly contemporary appearance – only the locomotive seems to have seen better days. No 45041 *Royal Tank Regiment* was built as part of a Crewe Works batch in 1962, and was numbered D53 until changed under the 1973 TOPS computer renumbering scheme. The location is South Brent, one time junction for the Kingsbridge branch, and the date 17 September 1982. *(Rodney Lissenden)*
Pentax 6×7   150mm
Agfa CT18   1/500, f4

Right. Scarcely overworked on this occasion is 45048 *The Royal Marines* at Dainton with a small up freight on 17 August 1983. Better known in the old days as D70, a Crewe product of 1960, this was a lifelong Midland locomotive until taken over by Holbeck (Leeds) in December 1973. *(Rodney Lissenden)*
Pentax 6×7   105mm
Agfa CT18   1/500, f4

Opposite. Deep in Cornwall's Fowey valley, 45012 leaves Lostwithiel on 17 September 1983 with the mixed-rake 0920 Liverpool-Penzance. Built as D108 at Crewe in 1961, this locomotive drifted from one depot to another until contractions in Peak maintenance arrangements deposited it at Tinsley. By the date of this picture the number 108 had reappeared at No 1 end. (*Hugh Ballantyne*)
Leica M4-2   90mm
Summicron   Kodachrome 25
1/250, f2.8-4

Left. Four china clay trainloads are a reassuring sight in the yards at Lostwithiel, once Great Western, now part of the Cornish Railways empire. Taken from the hilltop looking north, an unidentified Class 45/1 hurries through on the 0920 Liverpool-Penzance on a brilliantly sunlit first day of March 1984. (*John Chalcraft*)
Mamiya 645   210mm
Agfa R100S   1/500, f4.5

Opposite Top. A far cry from St Pancras duties! Stone traffic from the West Country is a vital part of the railway economy, but long climbs with 1000 tonnes or more in tow plays havoc with the motive power fleet. More powerful Class 56s and pairs of 37s now hold sway, but on 14 September 1979 it was the task of the 2500hp power unit inside 45007 to reverse these antiquated short-wheelbase tipplers into the reversing spur alongside the Berks and Hants line at Westbury before passing through the station to gain access to the SR. This locomotive started life as D119 from Crewe Works in October 1961, and was a regular on Midland Lines passenger work until transfer to the ER in 1973. (*Gavin Morrison*)
Pentax SP1000   Kodachrome 25   1/250, f3.5

Bottom. The common user aspect of Class 45/0s

nowadays is typified by this view of Toton's 45075 grinding through Stoke Gifford towards Bristol Parkway with yet another stone train from nearby Tytherington quarry on 10 July 1981. Needless to say there is little alternative use on a day like this for a Peak that still has an operational steam-heat boiler. Built as D132 at the end of 1961, 45075's future looked insecure at the end of 1984 because of its poor mechanical order and another lull in major works repairs. (*Geoff Cann*)
Mamiya 645   80mm Sekor C   Ektachrome 64 1/500, f4

Above. There always has to be an exception to any rùle, and 45022 *Lytham St Annes* can claim double significance over two decades. First, this Peak delivered as D60 from Crewe in February 1962 is the only Class 45 named after a town, and

secondly along with 45013 was in 1984 given a special livery that might have been nice new, but in the class's twilight years only helped emphasise its general weariness. Note the white cab surrounds and grilles, and bodyside stripe as it makes the familiar departure from Newton Abbot with the 0914 Blackpool-Penzance on 28 July 1984.

One of D60's most significant achievements was to haul the final Edinburgh-St Pancras sleeper service over the Waverley route on 5 January 1969, notably suffering an extended halt at Newcastleton when the local vicar was arrested for obstruction after blocking the track, despite pleas from passengers including the present Liberal leader David Steel. (*David Rapson*)
Canon AE1   Kodachrome 64 1/500, f4.8

Right. Swinging from the relief to the main lines as it leaves Newport tunnel at Gaer Junction on 14 April 1982 is 46050, thoroughly predictable choice as motive power for the 1008 Newcastle-Cardiff service. It is late afternoon, and this late 1962-vintage Peak will be serviced at Canton depot prior to immediate despatch back to the North East. Built as D187, this Brush traction-motored machine spent ten months of 1981 mothballed at Swindon, survived six more months after this picture, and at least another two years in the scraplines. Compare the view with Page 45. *(John Chalcraft) Mamiya 645 80mm Agfa R100S*

Opposite. The 138 tons that make up a Class 45 on rigid plate-frame bogies restrict the type's use to main lines, or secondary routes that prosper with heavy coal, Railfreight or steel traffic. Despite its weight a wide knowledge by crews up and down the country make the Peak a useful machine for almost every duty. This is 45068, which since being built as D118 at Crewe Works in the autumn of 1961 has always been the responsibility of Nottingham area depots. That meant little on 11 May 1983, however, when it was borrowed for an eastbound ballast working between Margam and Bridgend in South Wales. It is seen here sauntering through Pencoed. *(Mrs D A Robinson) Pentax 6×7 Ektachrome 200 1/1000, f4.5-5.6*

Peaks across the Border

Opposite. Did they ever look better than this? Split headcode Class 45 Peak D16 displays the final version of green livery, without off-white lower bodyside stripe or side grilles at Carlisle on 5 June 1967, prior to departure on the up 'Waverley'. The comparative lateness of the green repaint is also emphasised by the trailing rake of blue and grey Mark 1 stock. D16 was unique amongst the Class 45s in undergoing the transition to TOPs computerisation without pain – by sheer coincidence its new number is 45016. Built at Derby at the end of 1960, its duties in 1984 were from Toton.
(Derek Cross)
Linhof Technika   100mm Zeiss
Agfa CT18 Professional   1/250

Left. Many say the Scottish border counties never recovered from the grievous loss of the Waverley route on 5 January 1969, and only vast grass-covered embankments, cuttings, platform edges and long, long tunnels remain for the railway rambler. Views such as this have gone for ever – Heriot, a lonely Waverley route station some 15 miles south-east of Edinburgh, witnessed D114 at speed on a northbound Bathgate car train on 3 November 1965. As for the Crewe-built locomotive, it was still active in 1984 as 45066, operating from Toton.
(Derek Cross)
Rolleiflex 66
80mm Zeiss Planar
Agfa CT18 Professional   1/250

Below. Glasgow Central – the interim years. Don't be mistaken by the wires, they only served the domestic Scottish suburban system from 1962 when 'Blue Train' EMUs supplanted BR Standard 2-6-4Ts, but were isolated until the West Coast Main Line was connected up in 1974. This is Class 46 No 139, also in interim blue livery style with operational headcode on a Glasgow-Sheffield service on 12 January 1970.

Built by Derby workshops in 1961, this loco migrated from the London Midland to Western Regions in later years, and was scrapped at Swindon as 46002 in October 1984.
(Derek Cross)
Rolleiflex 66   80mm Zeiss Planar
Agfa CT18 Professional   1/250

Right. Millerhill yard, Edinburgh lost much of its raison d'être with the axing of the Waverley route from Carlisle in 1969, its foundations barely set. Thus, the Class 46s have always been part of this wasted rail landscape, and this was No 187 (later 46050) on a train of tanks for Thornaby on Tees on 11 March 1972. This locomotive was withdrawn ten years later and broken up at Swindon – see Page 40.
(David M Cross)

The Midland route to Scotland

Above. The 'Thames-Clyde Express' could be relied upon to produce a Peak throughout the 1960s, mostly an example from Derby depot. Five-year-old D20 still looked smart in its original green paintwork with white body stripe and bodyside grilles on 25 May 1966, coasting through the massive yard complex that once surrounded Wortley Junction, a stone's throw from the centre of Leeds and junction for the Harrogate and Skipton routes. D20, built at Derby in 1961, lost its split headcodes soon after renumbering to 45013, but was still considered a passenger locomotive as late as Spring 1984, when it was called into works for light overhaul and steam-heat boiler repairs. *(Gavin Morrison) Contaflex 50mm Tessar Agfa CT18 1/500, f3.5*

Right. On 3 August 1967 it was sister D26 on the southbound 'Thames-Clyde Express', still in original green livery style with grey bodyside stripe, and later small yellow warning panel, nicely framed by two signals having just crossed Ribblehead viaduct. Into the mid-1980s, the expresses have been diverted, the viaduct is to be singled for fear of collapse, and the locomotive, now 45020, is a freight-only machine based at Tinsley. *(Barrie Walker)*

46

An eye for a good photograph had to be combined with plenty of patience, a good map and a strong constitution to get this masterpiece, No 45143 *5th Royal Inniskilling Dragoon Guards* crossing Smardale viaduct on the Settle and Carlisle route with the 0907 Leeds-Carlisle on 18 January 1984. By this time, the Peaks' only duties on this threatened route were "local" services, few coaches but loaded to the brim with tourists out for a "last look" at this legendary route. *(Hugh Ballantyne)*
Leica M4-2   Summicron 50mm   Kodachrome 25 1/500, f2

Another Settle and Carlisle snow picture, and another look at the 0907 Leeds-Carlisle, this time passing through the deep cuttings at Dentdale on 7 January 1984. A dual-brake, electric-heat Class 45/1 is again somewhat over-generous for such a working, but 45109's displacement from the Midland Main Line by HSTs did leave Class 45 operating staff with a lot of spare capacity to fill. This locomotive was built as D85 at Crewe in 1961. (*Les Nixon*)
Nikon F 85mm Nikkor Kodachrome 25 1/250, f3.2

Left. The Midland Railway signal cabin, the purple and green backdrop, the stone walls . . . perfect setting for a 'Patriot' or 'Royal Scot' 4-6-0. By 1982, the best you could hope for on the 1030 Nottingham-Glasgow through Ais Gill was 45064, a Crewe-built Peak of 1961 vintage. The service that offered buffet facilities over the S and C is no more – all through services have been diverted via the WCML. As for 45064, this locomotive was, in 1967 as D105, the first Peak to receive blue livery, oddly with a small yellow warning panel. (*Mrs D A Robinson*)
Pentax 6×7   Ektachrome 200   1/500, f6.3

The later years
Above. A minor branch line from Grantham to Sleaford achieved greater importance after the massive Lincolnshire lines shutdown of 4 October 1970 and Ancaster station confines now shake with the procession of excursion trains using the only available route to the now remote but still lucrative outpost of Skegness. Passing Ancaster on 10 September 1983 was ETH-equipped 45125 on the 1105 Skegness-Sheffield. This loco started life as D123 from Crewe in 1961. Note the sidings – for all its remoteness Ancaster still sports a little grain traffic. (*Rodney Lissenden*)
Pentax 6×7   150mm   Ektachrome 200   1/500, f6.3

Top. The rundown of the Class 45 fleet was well underway by March 1983, when BR took us all by surprise and decided to put a handful through works for overhaul. Rundown of Derby locomotive shops by then was well advanced, so Crewe got the work instead. Outcome was sights like this – a freshly repainted 45009 (*ex-*D37) at Aintree, Liverpool on an Orrell Park-Fazakerly pw duty on 15 May. Withdrawals resumed in October 1984 however with 45002/23/43/50 to be dismantled for spares. (*Fred Kerr*)
Pentax 6×7   90mm
Agfa R100S   1/250, f5.6

Right. An interesting duty for the now down-graded Peaks is the Greater Manchester Council 'Binliner' service from Dean Lane near Newton Heath to the Wimpey Waste Management landfill site at Appley Bridge on the Southport-Wigan line. Inaugurated in mid-1981, the service soon passed from Class 25 and 40 haulage to Class 45/0s — and this was 45013 (D20, first of the 1961 Derby build) about to return from Appley Bridge with the return empties on 3 November 1982. (*R T Osborne*)
Canon AE1   200mm zoom at 150mm
Kodachrome 64   1/250, f5.6

007 makes his getaway! Hardly James Bond stuff though, as 45007 rumbles through Horbury and Ossett with an engineer's ballast train bound for Healey Mills in the bitter snow of 25 January 1984. By this time one of the Tinsley (Sheffield) fleet, 45007 typified the class's later years in having its train-heat boiler taken out of use, but not removed. In more demanding days, it was a regular sight on 'Thames-Clyde Express' duties, having been built as D119 at Crewe Works at the end of 1961. *(Les Nixon)*
Nikon F   85mm Nikkor   Kodachrome 25
1/250, f4.5

53

Left. A pleasing array of semaphore signals decorates the skyline of Scarborough, which may well end up as the final passenger stamping ground of the Class 45/1s, not guaranteed a long life now that full-scale national electrification will free Brush Class 47s to replace them. A good sunny day on the beach was the attraction facing the passengers in this 0705 ex-Liverpool service approaching the Falsgrave platform on 18 June 1983. Locomotive is 45146, which started life as

D66 from Crewe Works in early 1962, and was never allocated anywhere but former Midland Railway depots. (*John Chalcraft*)
Mamiya 645   80mm   Agfa R100S

Above. Huttons Ambo is a favourite spot a mile south of Malton on the Scarborough-York route built by the North Eastern Railway, and a secure haven for ETH-fitted Class 45/1s. Haulage for the 1600 Scarborough-Liverpool service on 16

April 1984 was 45143, the Peak with arguably the most incomprehensible name – *5th Royal Inniskilling Dragoon Guards*, a mouthful attached at a St Pancras in 1964 to a two-year-old Crewe-built D62 that was certainly never intended to work this sort of seaside trip! (*David Stacey*)
Pentax K1000   50mm   Kodachrome 25 1/250, f4

Above. By 1984 use of electric-heat Class 45/1s on North Wales-East Coast self-enclosed diagrams meant these erstwhile Toton-based locomotives were spending so long away from their home depot that others such as Allerton (Liverpool) and Longsight were building up their own stocks of spares to keep them running. Its Midland Line days now a memory, No 45148 (D130, Crewe 1961) was motive power for the 1732 departure from Bangor to York and Scarborough on 9 June 1984. *(Barry Plues)*
Pentax SP1000 50mm Kodachrome 64 1/250, f8

Right. Transfer of Class 45/1s to North Wales services in large numbers in 1982 after their displacement from the Midland Main Line was slow to gain acceptance from enthusiasts who mourned the demise from the route of the older and noisier English Electric Class 40s. The Peaks got on with the job quietly and efficiently, and doubtless their big moments are yet to come. 45117 is the computer number of this loco arriving at Llandudno Junction with the 1110 Scarborough-Bangor on 17 August 1984, disguising the original identity of D35, delivered new from Derby Works to Derby depot in July

1961. This loco pioneered use of the type on the Western Region following its immediate transfer to Bristol once acceptance trials had been completed. Training on Peaks of WR crews had begun earlier that year when D93 (45057) was borrowed for the purpose from the LMR by Bath Road. *(Ken Harris)*
Yashica TL Electro X 80mm Zeiss Kodachrome 25 1/500, f2.8

Opposite. Photography of Peaks among the Peaks has been at its best since the cascading of so many BR Sulzer Type 4s to the North West-East Coast routes, especially via Standedge. Colour work requires particular expertise, as no darkroom technique can rectify a poorly composed or exposed effort. This one is perfect – 45117 again on the 1605 Liverpool-Newcastle nears Greenfield, just north of Manchester, on 2 July 1983. *(John S Whiteley)*
Pentax 6×7 150mm Ektachrome 200 1/500, f6.3

Left. Travel by train on the Leeds-Manchester route cannot provide the view of the Saddleworth Viaduct offered to the photographer from this high vantage point. It's a good place nowadays for Peaks as well, and 2 July 1983 was a typical day when 45115 was employed on the 1710 York-Manchester. Older readers may recall 45115 as D81, a product of Crewe Works in December 1960, and apart from a three-year spell at Cricklewood, a Nottingham-based machine ever since. *(John S Whiteley)*
Pentax 6×7 Ektachrome 200 1/500, f5.6

Overleaf left. The Peaks that used to rattle through Chinley on Derby-Manchester expresses are still seen on what is left of this former Midland main line, but principal duties nowadays are stone trains from Tunstead to Northwich. The whole area nowadays has a general air of dereliction with lifted track and half demolished stations. 45001, working such a limestone duty on 3 April 1984, may be the lowest numbered Class 45, but its TOPS computer number conceals its true identity as D13, built at Derby in 1960. *(John S Whiteley)*
Pentax SP 135mm Takumar Kodachrome 64 1/250, f6.3

Right. A Peak leaves home. 45019 leaves Tinsley yard with an early afternoon Speedlink service on 9 February 1984. The picture is filled with miles of sidings, but there doesn't appear to be a great deal going on! The locomotive is also in a general state of decay, but its dual-braked state made it as useful a machine as any that this last surviving heavy maintenance depot in Yorkshire can muster. 45019, plain and simple D33 when delivered from Derby in June 1961, was tossed back and forth between the London Midland, North Eastern and Western Regions before settling in this area in 1972. If mechanical failure does not get to it first, the East Coast electrification will see its demise. *(Les Nixon)*
Pentax 6×7 105mm Takumar Ektachrome 200 1/250, f6.3

In works

Below. General overhaul of a BR locomotive involves literally reducing it to its basic components, which are distributed across the works for either repair or replacement from the stores. Work had just started on 45019 at Derby (it was built there as D33 in 1961) on the occasion of the Open Day on 6 September 1980, with removal of bogies and power unit. Note the non-standard headcode modification carried on one end for a couple of months. *(Gordon Bird)*
Fujica 605 55mm Fujichrome R100
1/30, f4

Above. The Peaks became a vital part of Derby Works throughput after the end of steam, and the rundown of the class in recent years has posed a major threat to the workforce. From 1973, 50 of the Class 45s were selected for heavy overhaul and equipping with electric train heating equipment to haul more modern Mark 2 stock on the Midland Main Line, and this patchwork quilt in works on 29 May 1974 would emerge as 45128 (built Crewe 1961 as D113). *(Hugh Ballantyne)*
Leica M3 50mm Summicron Kodachrome II
1/60, f5.6-8

Below. The repaint of old soldier 44008 *Penyghent* for the 9 June 1979 Toton Open Day was without question the smartest on any single Peak since the transition to blue livery started by D105 back in 1966. That beauty was marred somewhat by the addition of a white roof and broad stripe on the lower bodyside panels for the final workings that preceded the 44s' final withdrawal with 44004/7 on 30 September 1980. The story of 44008 does not end there: it was towed further north than ever before for preservation on the Strathspey Railway at Boat of Garten. (*Fred Kerr*)
Canon FTB   85mm   Ektachrome 200
1/250, f6.3

Above. Toton depot's affection for the Class 44s helped extend their expected life by up to ten years! Best of the bunch when the end finally came in November 1980 was undoubtedly 44004 Great Gable, which spent its last few months in traffic back in its old green livery. Preservation was thus less of a surprise, and restoration as D4 at the Midland Railway Trust centre at Butterley has been most thorough. Gone were the disfiguring full yellow ends by the time this picture was taken on 5 June 1982. (*Paul Johnston*)
Pentax ME Super   50mm   Kodachrome 64
1/250, f8

Peaks preserved

D8 (44008) *Penyghent*, named Derby, December 1959. *(Barry Nicolle)*

D53 (45041) *Royal Tank Regiment*, named 24 September 1964. *(Hugh Ballantyne)*

D53 (45143) *5th Royal Inniskilling Dragoon Guards*, named St Pancras, 30 November 1964. *(Paul Johnston)*

D71 (45049) *The Staffordshire Regiment (The Prince of Wales')*, named 20 May 1966. *(David Stacey)*

D89 (45006) *Honourable Artillery Company*, named Broad Street, 9 June 1965. *(Howard Johnston)*

D100 (45060) *Sherwood Forester*, named Derby, 23 September 1961. *(Hugh Ballantyne)*

Nameplates

To the layman, the nickname 'Peak' when attached to a Class 45 or 46 locomotive may appear incongruous in the extreme. After the christening of Class 44s D1-D10 as the highest (and most easily pronounced) of English and Welsh mountains, the name stuck for their successors. In the 1960s vogue, ceremonies were set up at London and provincial stations to enable regiments to be immortalised on the most recently ex-works locomotive – hence the apparently indiscriminate choice. In all 26 Class 45 locomotives were named, as well as Class 46 No 46026. Many of the names came off steam precessors such as LMS 4-6-0s, and that also explains the anomaly of 45022 (D60) *Lytham St Annes*, which formerly graced a 'Patriot' class loco. In recent years, either crests or complete plates have been removed.